The Insider's Guide to Micro Hedge Funds

The financial strategy and tactics used by the One Percent to become wealthy and rich and how you can become one of them too!

I0503515

The Insider's Guide to Micro Hedge Funds
By
Roman de Caesar

The Insider's Guide to Micro Hedge Funds
Copyright 2017 by Roman de Caesar

ISBN-13: 978-1542379557   ISBN-10: 1542379555

Published by: Spencer Marlowe

Printed in the United States of America

Aufidena Financial
1205 Johnson Ferry Road
Suite 136 – 212
Marietta, Georgia 30068.

Interior Design by Spencer Marlowe
Cover Design by Spencer Marlowe

TABLE OF CONTENTS

A QUOTE BY WARREN BUFFETT

"It's nice to have a lot of money, but you know, you don't want to keep it around forever. I prefer buying things. Otherwise, it's a little like saving sex for your old age."

— Warren Buffett

ACKNOWLEDGEMENTS

To those of you who have encouraged me and inspired me, and stood by me: I am eternally in your debt:

Ms. Annie Jennings of Annie Jennings PR & Radio

Ms. Helen Chang of Author Bridge Media Group

Mr. Warren Buffett of Berkshire-Hathaway

DEDICATION

This book is dedicated to the billions of people who have lived and died, and those who are alive today, who through no fault of their own have been denied the opportunity to learn, understand, believe, embrace and apply their God given abilities, gifts, skills and talents for the purpose of making the world a more beautiful and prosperous place to live in.

It is dedicated to you, because you were purposely misled by institutions you were told to respect and trust, with disinformation, misinformation and useless information in order to deliberately keep you enslaved and prevent you from fulfilling your potential to become wealthy and rich.

Obtain, therefore, the knowledge and wisdom required in order to set yourself free from economic, religious and social enslavement and tyranny: use the knowledge and wisdom found in this book and others like it to experience a wonderful life, heal the world, and bring a new age of enlightenment into it, whereby if Voltaire were alive today, he would say to you:

"Well done! Well done indeed!"

INTRODUCTION

Precision Investment Opportunities at Your Command

Few people possess the knowledge and the wisdom to comprehend and envision how human behavior directly impacts and influences consumer buying decisions. And even fewer people possess the knowledge and the wisdom to comprehend and envision how human behavior also directly impacts and influences financial investment choices. Yet, those few, those intelligent few, who have learned, understood, believed, embraced and applied a definitive knowledge of human behavior in relation to human wants versus human needs are today the wealthiest and richest people living on the planet. They are the one percent.

I want you to read that paragraph again. Go on: read it.

Few people possess the knowledge and the wisdom to comprehend and envision how human behavior directly impacts and influences consumer buying decisions. And even fewer people possess the knowledge and the wisdom to comprehend and envision how human behavior also directly impacts and influences financial investment choices. Yet, those few, those intelligent few, who have learned, understood, believed, embraced and applied a definitive knowledge of human behavior in relation to human wants versus human needs are today the wealthiest and richest people living on the planet. They are the one percent.

Now, I want you to read it again. Don't stop now: read it very slowly, and very carefully.

Few people possess the knowledge and the wisdom to comprehend and envision how human behavior directly impacts and influences consumer buying decisions. And even fewer people possess the knowledge and the wisdom to comprehend and envision how human behavior also directly impacts and influences financial investment choices. Yet, those few, those intelligent few, who have learned, understood, believed, embraced and applied a definitive knowledge of human behavior in relation to human wants versus human needs are today the wealthiest and richest people living on the planet. They are the one percent.

In fact, after you read it a third time, I want you, in your own handwriting, to take a piece of paper and pen (no pencil please), and very neatly write down that paragraph exactly as it is written here in this book. Why?

Because that paragraph, comprised of three sentences and exactly eighty six words contains the most important wisdom regarding wealth and riches you will ever read. It isn't a mystery: it isn't "secret." And it certainly isn't some kind of "Da Vinci Code." It is however, the foundational principle behind Micro Hedge Funds.

And, as you read this book, it is my hope that you will learn, understand, believe, embrace and apply the knowledge and the wisdom contained in that paragraph, because if and when you do, there will no longer be any barriers to any financial goal you desire to achieve through the use of Micro Hedge Funds.

So, if you are ready to be truly educated, read on, because I have a true story to tell you: it is an amazing story!

SETTING THE STAGE

An Amazing Story

On November 17, 2016 Julien's Auctions auctioned off one the most famous dresses owned by one of the most gorgeous actresses of the 20th century. The actress's name is Marilyn Monroe; and, the dress that was auctioned that night in Los Angeles, California was the famous (or infamous if you prefer) "Happy Birthday, Mr. President" Dress (i.e., the "Dress")

For those of you who may not be familiar with the woman or the Dress, it is important for you to pay attention to this story, because Marilyn and her Dress illustrates the method behind the power of how Micro Hedge Funds work: this story is instrumental in helping you to learn, understand, believe, embrace and apply the financial methods and principles of the Micro Hedge Fund Matrix.

The Dress was made by couture fashion designer Jean Louis for Marilyn: the materials used to construct the Dress consisted of a sheer and flesh-colored marquisette fabric, with 2,500 shimmering rhinestones sewn into it. Marilyn purchased the Dress in 1962 for $1,440.33 USD, and today, taking into account inflation, that same dress would cost, in 2017 dollars, $11,355.80 USD.

Marilyn wore the Dress on stage once: she wore it at Madison Square Garden in New York City in May of 1962 when she gave one of the sexist performances of her life: in front of the cameras, and in front of a packed audience, she sang "Happy Birthday" to President John F. Kennedy (i.e., "JFK").

Although many people living at that time didn't know it, it is widely known today that JFK and Marilyn had an extra marital affair prior to and during JFK's first and only term in office as President of the United States of America.

And, since 1962, which is also the year that Marilyn died, the Dress has had several owners, and has been sold at auction several times, each time being sold for a significant profit. For example, in 1999, the Dress sold at auction in New York City for 1.26 Million USD. And, most recently, on November 17th, the dress was purchased by an anonymous bidder for $ 4.8 Million USD.

Now, if you are thinking to yourself...

..."Who in their right mind would need to purchase a dress that was worn once, by a dead actress, who is claimed to have had an extra marital affair with JFK...for 4.8 Million Dollars, when that same dress is only worth $11,355.80?"...

...then my friend, you have just demonstrated beyond a shadow of a doubt that you do not possess the knowledge or the wisdom required to become wealthy and rich by any means or method.

However, don't be dismayed and don't be angry: this book possesses, at high level, that knowledge and wisdom, and if you have the aptitude to learn, understand, believe, embrace and apply what this book teaches, you can change your life and your financial fortune for the better.

So, if you're ready, let us look at the factors, define their meaning and learn, understand, believe, embrace and apply the methods, principles, values and virtues that made the Dress an incredible Micro Hedge Fund financial investment choice opportunity.

OUR MODIS OPERANDI

What makes us tick?

What makes us "tick" when it comes to using or acquiring wealth and riches? How do we as human beings operate when it comes to creating wealth and acquiring riches?

Have you ever asked yourself these questions? Have you ever answered any of these questions correctly?

You see, ninety-nine percent of the world's population has never asked or answered these questions, but the one percent who have asked these questions, and who have also answered them correctly based upon a careful analysis of facts, evidence and logic are the same one percent that possess ninety-nine percent of the world's wealth and riches today, and that's a fact.

"How?" you ask?

Let's begin by re-examining the first sentence of that all, important paragraph:

Few people possess the knowledge and the wisdom to comprehend and envision how human behavior directly impacts and influences consumer buying decisions.

At this moment in time, whether you like it or not or whether you believe it or not, your consumer buying decisions are driven by your intuitive, instinctive and intrinsic desire to achieve ever increasing amounts of three things daily in your life. Those three things are:

1. Power
2. Prestige (i.e., Status); and,
3. Social Standing (i.e., Class)

Now, let's define each of these three words in the context of their importance in relation to the Micro Hedge Fund Matrix.

Power: a person's ability to get their way despite the resistance of others, particularly in their ability to engage or inspire economic and social change (or, said another way, the ability to wield considerable personal power over the mind, will and emotions of others regardless of what others wants or needs may be).

Prestige: a person's amount or level of social honor and social popularity in a society.

Social Standing: a person's economic position in a society, based upon birth and individual achievement measured by the acquisition of wealth and riches.

However, and to use an analogy, Power, Prestige and Social Standing are only the visible, upper half of the "iceberg." What lies beneath the surface, hidden in the depths of the souls (i.e., the mind, the will and the emotions) of man and mankind is substantially larger, and more important to consider.

What am I referring to?

To be or not to be...that is the question.

FACT: consumer buying decisions are driven by every person's desire for Power, Prestige and Social Standing. It doesn't matter whether we are talking about buying Band-Aids or Bugatti automobiles: your consumer buying decisions are based upon your desire for more Power, Prestige and Social Standing every day of your life.

FACT: when a person exercises their consumer buying decisions, they want to experience the feeling that the act increases, even if only slightly, the amount of Power, Prestige and Social Standing they possess and will experience moving forward into the future.

FACT: the only people on the earth who don't care about Power, Prestige and Social Standing are dead.

Think about it: with so many, less expensive Generic products on the market shelves today, why do you always reach for and buy the Brand Name product instead of the Generic product? Or, when you buy the no-name, less expensive Generic product instead of the Brand Name product you can afford, why don't you feel as happy, glad or as satisfied as you do when you buy the Brand Name product at the higher price?

Think about it: with so many cars on the road today, why do you always find yourself wanting a better, newer model than the model you are driving today? Or, when you are driving your car, and find yourself at a stop light sitting next to that new or used Audi, BMW or Lexus luxury import you don't own, why do you find yourself aching to have that Audi, BMW or Lexus for yourself?

No pun intended, but the truth is you're driven: you're driven everyday of your life to increase your Power, your Prestige and your Social Standing, even if it's just a little bit. And this is a good thing, because when this happens, it means you're alive and growing as a human being. Personally, I refer to this as "Dignity Building" when it is done appropriately and constructively. When it isn't, I call it self-destruction.

Unfortunately, for ninety-nine percent of the population, they see this as being a "bad thing", because they've been programmed to accept the "bad thing" lie as the "gospel" truth. From an economic perspective, you are taught that growth is "greedy." From a religious perspective, you are taught that growth is "sinful." From a social (or cultural perspective) you are taught that this is being "selfish." And by the way, this "gospel" of perversion is reinforced by the "experts", your "superiors", your "peers" and your "subordinates" every day, and in every way, because far be it that you should escape the mundane and the mediocre and fulfill your potential as a human being when they can't. Like the old adage says, "Misery loves company."

So, when it comes to you, you do whatever you can in order to refrain from being perceived as being "greedy", "sinful" or "selfish", because you have four distinct needs: the need to be recognized, accepted, included and respected by the very same "experts, "superiors", "peers" and "subordinates" who, by your invitation or through no choice of your own, are a part of your everyday reality.

And in the process, you sabotage your very soul and your very existence by starving yourself of the consumer buying decision experiences that help you grow as a person and make you whole as a human being. And, when you deny yourself these Dignity Building experiences from a consumer buying decision perspective, you automatically, and with catastrophic effect, prevent yourself from making any financial investment choices that are worthy of your true self.

Let me assure you that the one percent of the population, who have the majority of the world's wealth and riches haven't been, don't and won't succumb to this diseased form of being or thinking, but rather appreciate and acknowledge the need to grow by exercising their consumer buying decisions in ways that are constructive and help them acquire more Power, Prestige and Social Standing every day of their life, because from an economic perspective they see this as a "personal duty." From a religious perspective, they see this as a "righteous obligation." From a social (or cultural perspective) they see this as a "moral responsibility."

And, the more times they apply their Dignity Building experiences from a consumer buying decision perspective, they automatically, and with dramatically profitable results, constantly improve their financial investment choices, which build their wealth and their riches every day.

Ladies and gentlemen: this is the difference between the "Haves" and the "Have Nots." This is the difference between the one percent who live in peace and prosperity and the ninety-nine percent who live in their own hell.

The question is simply this: which group do you belong to? Do you have a life of peace and prosperity? Or, do you live in your own, man (or mankind) made hell?

If "hell" is your answer, you may want to consider a Paradigm Shift, but before we do that, let's step into the Matrix.

The Matrix

From this point forward I want you to think about every consumer buying decision and every financial investment choice you make as being exercised within what we will call the Micro Hedge Fund Matrix, or "Matrix" for short; and, the Matrix has an X-Axis and a Y-Axis.

For the purposes of this discussion we'll refer to the X-Axis as Human Emotion, or "Emotion." We've spoken about Emotion previously, and will now define it as being comprised and characterized by the definitions of Power, Prestige and Social Standing we mentioned earlier.

In contrast, the Y-Axis we'll call the Financial Object, or "Object." And, in this section, we'll define the words that comprise the characteristics of an Object.

But first, let's revisit what makes us tick: what is our Modis operandi, but this time from the perspective of financial investment choices, and not consumer buying preferences.

How?

Let's begin by re-examining the second sentence of that all, important paragraph:

And even fewer people possess the knowledge and the wisdom to comprehend and envision how human behavior also directly impacts and influences financial investment choices.

What makes a good financial investment choice? There are many answers to that question, but for the purpose of discussing the Micro Hedge Fund Matrix, let's agree to adopt the following definition used by the one percent, who possess ninety-nine percent of the world's wealth and riches:

A good financial investment choice is one that empowers and enables an individual person to increase their wealth and / or riches substantially, and as quickly as possible, while also increasing their Power, their Prestige and their Social Standing.

With that definition adopted, let's discuss the Y-Axis; or, in other words, let's identify the four attributes that wealthy and rich people use to analyze, evaluate and validate what makes a good Object to pursue as a financial investment choice.

As with consumer buying decisions, the financial investment choices of the wealthy and the rich have always (and I mean HAVE ALWAYS) been driven by their intuitive, instinctive and intrinsic desire to acquire Objects that are:

1. Valuable;
2. Unique;
3. Powerful; and
4. Nostalgic

No matter how you viewed or defined these four words in the past, I am asking you to now erase those views and definitions from your mind, and prepare to learn what they really mean by studying their correct definitions.

Valuable: an Object's degree of desirability and importance, which is based upon its ability and / or capability to enhance and / or redefine a person's Power, Prestige and Social Standing while appreciating in economic value.

Unique: the state and the condition of an Object (that is either one of a kind or unlike anything else) that when possessed by an owner, enhances and / or redefines the owners Power, Prestige or Social Standing.

Powerful: an Object whose value and uniqueness when possessed by the owner creates in the mind of the owner and society the belief that the Object adds to the Power, Prestige and Social Standing of the owner in a significant and enviable way.

Nostalgic: an Object possessed by the owner that increases the Power, Prestige and Social Standing of the owner but also redefines for the owner the meaning, importance and value of their life while they possess the Object.

With this in the forefront of your mind, the Matrix looks like this:

THE MATRIX			
Emotion / Object	Power	Prestige	Social Standing
Valuable			
Unique			
Powerful			
Nostalgic			

PARADIGM SHIFT

From Need to Want

Like most people I have my passions: I love to fly, I love to drive and I love to sail: I love to jet-ski, snow ski and drive my powerboat as if I were a drug smuggler on his way to Key West. I enjoy doing these things (recreationally, of course) because each of these passions helps me to stay sharp, fit and sexy. And, although I don't have many friends, I know many people who share the same passions as I do, and some of them are wealthier and richer than I am, and can afford to purchase more expensive "toys" than I have today. And, that's OK, because as I grow and fulfill my potential as a human being, I'll reach that level of wealth and riches in the near future, and upgrade my vehicles and equipment accordingly. Until then, I'll simply enjoy the journey to that destination.

But in the past, when I have shared my experiences and stories about these One Percenters (as I like to call them) with people who, for lack of a better term represent the Ninety-Nine Percenters, I'm always deluged with questions from these people in a critical and judgmental tone of voice that sets one nerves on edge, like finger nails scraping a chalk board:

Who needs to spend half a million dollars on a Rolls Royce?

Who needs to spend a quarter million dollars on a 7-carat diamond engagement ring?

Who needs to spend $800.00 on a canoe? Hell, nobody even uses canoes anymore!!!

As you can imagine, I no longer share my experiences or stories with people who represent the Ninety-Nine Percenters: it's like casting pearls before swine.

However, let me ask you a familiar question:

Who needs to spend 4.8 Million Dollars for a dress that was worn once, by a dead actress, who is believed to have had an extra marital affair with JFK, when that same dress, if it were made today with the same pattern and the same materials would only cost $11,355.80 to make? In fact, who would want to buy a dress like that for $11,355.80? Hell, most women can't even fit into that size dress anymore!!!

Listen to me very carefully: wealthy and rich people do not buy things because they need them: they buy them, because they want them! They buy things, which are Valuable, Unique, Powerful and Nostalgic, because by doing so, they increase their Power, Prestige and Social Standing, and thereby grow and fulfill their individual, human potential.

Please recognize this: the number one common denominator among wealthy and rich people is their strong, self-awareness of the difference between needs (that when satisfied do nothing to increase Power, Prestige or Social Standing) and wants (that when satisfied increase Power, Prestige and Social Standing dramatically).

How do I know that this is true? Now, it is time to re-examine the third and last sentence of that all, important paragraph:

Yet, those few, those intelligent few, who have learned, understood, believed, embraced and applied a definitive knowledge of human behavior in relation to human wants versus human needs are today the wealthiest and richest people living on the planet. They are the one percent.

The "One Percenters" have made the Paradigm Shift. They do not focus on getting their needs met: rather, they focus solely on getting their wants fulfilled, which guarantees that any need they have will be satisfied as well.

They prepare, plan and act this way, because they recognize that real living is achieved only through personal growth: they recognize that they are on the fast track to personal growth (i.e., the growth of their spirit, their soul and their body) and human fulfillment, and that it requires wealth and riches in order to power them and propel them to higher levels of self-awareness through Dignity Building.

This concept is timeless: many, smart people from the past knew this, and spent their lives trying to get their contemporaries to make the paradigm shift. Aristotle knew this. Voltaire knew this. Dale Carnegie knew this and spent his entire life writing books and speaking about this to no avail. And, before Dale Carnegie there was Wallace D. Wattles, who in the 19th & 20th centuries wrote about the "Science of Getting Rich", only to have it fall on deaf ears.

Where Aristotle, Voltaire, Carnegie, Wattles and many others failed in their attempts to enlighten people regarding the acquisition of wealth and riches was that they did not have the financial instrument available to help them illustrate and explain how one can prepare, plan and act in order to increase their Power, their Prestige and their Social Standing through financial investment choices that are Valuable, Unique, Powerful and Nostalgic.

This is where the Micro Hedge Fund Matrix becomes invaluable not only as an educational tool but as the method to change your financial fortune.

FINANCIAL INVESTMENT CHOICES

Micro Hedge Funds versus Radicalized Hedge Funds

The earliest, traditional hedge funds were created during the late 19th and early 20th centuries as a financial investment fund to pool capital from closely knit individual investors for the purpose of investing those funds within a narrow band of common assets using generally accepted accounting & finance principles. Barriers to entry did not exist, and the funds pooled where managed by business professionals who not only had expertise in accounting, asset and financial management, but also experience with creating, managing and maintaining the types of assets included within the traditional hedge funds portfolio. During these early days, these traditional hedge funds performed very well, and became a valued financial instrument for building wealth and riches among all people from every walk of life.

But as the 20th century progressed, traditional hedge funds began to lose their respectability: criminal elements infiltrated the hedge fund industry, because they saw the potential to take advantage of this lightly regulated financial instrument for unlawful gains. Thus, and as a result of several financial scandals, traditional hedge funds came under greater scrutiny and became more regulated whereby only accredited individual investors or licensed institutional investors could participate in these funds, which now employed highly complicated portfolio building and risk mitigation techniques. In short, traditional hedge funds morphed into the hedge funds we have today, which I refer to as "Radicalized Hedge Funds."

In summary traditional hedge funds went from being very streamlined, very simple and very easily managed financial portfolios into Radicalized Hedge Funds, which are risk laden, highly over-regulated and highly speculative ventures, whose success rates were more a result of collaborative insider trading than practical application of financially sound principles and brilliantly savvy investing. This is why, during the first ten years of the 21th century, many of the previously rated, top Radicalized Hedge Fund management firms have and continue to report significant losses in their portfolios.

So it begs to question, if in the beginning when traditional hedge funds worked so well, wouldn't it be more preferable and more profitable to return to the old ways of those early days, while also maintaining the highest standards of ethics as well as financial performance? The answer is a resounding yes. And the way is found through learning, understanding, believing, embracing and applying the Micro Hedge Fund Matrix.

A Micro Hedge Fund is a return to doing hedge funds right: it incorporates all of the proven features and benefits found in traditional hedge funds but also possesses seven magnificent advantages that Radicalized Hedge Funds will never have.

I call them the "Magnificent Seven."

The Magnificent Seven

Micro Hedge Funds have more than seven, distinct advantages over their radicalized counterparts. However, and because this book is a primer, the intention of the author is to provide an accurate, but easily understood explanation of each of these seven, superior advantages. With that said, let's get started with the expectation that this is written for a wider audience other than experienced financial professionals, who may have picked up this book.

First, Financial Investment Focus: whereas Radical Hedge Funds invest in business entities, Micro Hedge Funds invest in one, particular Object only. This is significant, because it enables the Micro Hedge Fund manager to systematically and accurately (using generally accepted accounting principles and proven financial management techniques) measure and maximize Object performance while reducing risks to the absolute minimum possible.

Second, Insured, Secured & Collateralized: whereas Radical Hedge Funds only invest in business entities, Micro Hedge Funds invest in Objects, which are heavily insured, secured and collateralized to protect the interests of the Micro Hedge Fund Portfolio. This means that in case of damage or destruction of the Object, the interests of the Micro Hedge Fund are always covered, all of the time; and, in the event of damage or destruction to the Object, the speed and simplicity of reimbursing the Micro Hedge Fund and restoring the investment pool is significantly faster than a Radical Hedge Fund (i.e., less "Red Tape).

Third, Superior Portfolio Risk Management: whereas Radical Hedge Funds are exposed to multiple sources of varying risk types, and have no cap on the amount of money the overall Portfolio may pool or invest in proportion to the qualified or unqualified risks, a Micro Hedge Fund Portfolio's risk exposure is limited to the risk associated with the singular Object contained within that Object's own Portfolio. Further, each Portfolio has a cap proportionate to the estimated current and future value of the Object, which protects the interests of the investment pool engaged with the Object as its preferred, financial investment choice.

Fourth, Superior Portfolio Management: whereas Radical Hedge Funds are comprised of varying risk types and require complex and sophisticated methods to manage the potential risks of the overall Portfolio in the short and long term, Micro Hedge Funds need only employ Object-related risk models, which are much easier to construct, easy to understand, comfortable to manage and accurate to use in forecasting profitability during the entire Portfolio lifecycle. This is achieved because of the narrow focus of the Object, which represents a pinpoint precision financial investment choice while also understanding its unique set of identifiable, qualified risks.

Fifth, Pre-determined Portfolio Lifecycle: whereas Radical Hedge Funds are constructed to have a perpetual lifecycle based upon the assumption that the Portfolio will always remain profitable, Micro Hedge Fund Portfolios have a pre-determined entrance and exit strategy that coincides with and compliments the expectations of the Objects financial performance.

Sixth, Tangible versus Intangible: whereas Radical Hedge Funds can and usually do invest in both tangible and intangible assets, Micro Hedge Funds only invest in real, tangible assets, thus significantly reducing the potential risk of depreciation as a result of the intangible asset losing its value due to competitive challenges or regulatory pressures over time.

Seventh: Barriers to entry: whereas Radical Hedge Funds can only solicit and admit accredited investors and / or licensed investment institutions into its investment pool, Micro Hedge Funds can admit anyone regardless of financial net worth, physical location or prior experience exercising their financial investment choices.

All of these advantages are important: all of them are very meaningful. But of the seven listed here, the seventh advantage is quite possibly the most unique.

Obviously, everyone wants to know "how." We'll discuss the "how" as well as the "who", the "what", the "where", the "when" and the "why" later in this book.

But for now, let's revisit the Matrix.

THE MATRIX REVISITED

By now, you should have been able to learn, understand and believe the strength of the Micro Hedge Fund Matrix: specifically, you should have a firm, mental grasp of the following:

Few people possess the knowledge and the wisdom to comprehend and envision how human behavior directly impacts and influences consumer buying decisions.

Where does an understanding of this knowledge and wisdom reside?

1. *Power*
2. *Prestige (i.e., Status); and,*
3. *Social Standing (i.e., Class)*

And even fewer people possess the knowledge and the wisdom to comprehend and envision how human behavior also directly impacts and influences financial investment choices.

What is a good financial investment choice?

A good financial investment choice is one that empowers and enables an individual person to increase their wealth and / or riches substantially, and as quickly as possible, while also increasing their Power, their Prestige and their Social Standing.

What drives the financial investment choices of the wealthy and the rich?

...their intuitive, instinctive and intrinsic desire to acquire Objects that are:

1. *Valuable;*
2. *Unique;*
3. *Powerful; and*
4. *Nostalgic*

And how is this represented?

THE MATRIX			
Emotion / Object	Power	Prestige	Social Standing
Valuable			
Unique			
Powerful			
Nostalgic			

Yet, those few, those intelligent few, who have learned, understood, believed, embraced and applied a definitive knowledge of human behavior in relation to human wants versus human needs are today the wealthiest and richest people living on the planet. They are the one percent.

Who are the "One Percent" and what is their Modis operandi?

The "One Percenters" have made the Paradigm Shift. They do not focus on getting their needs met: rather, they focus solely on getting their wants fulfilled, which guarantees that any need they have will be satisfied as well.

They prepare, plan and act this way, because they recognize that real living is achieved only through personal growth: they recognize that they are on the fast track to personal growth (i.e., the growth of their spirit, their soul and their body) and human fulfillment, and that it requires wealth and riches in order to power them and propel them to higher levels of self-awareness through Dignity Building.

Now, if for any reason you have been unable to learn, understand or believe what you've been presented with thus far, I will ask you to please go back to the beginning of this book, and re-read all of the pages up and until this point. Because if you have not been able to learn, understand or believe the elementary components of the Micro Hedge Fund Matrix, the second half of this book will not make any sense to you.

However, if it does make sense to you, and you are ready to embrace and apply the Matrix, let's proceed.

Genius through Creative Simplicity

Mr. Burt Rutan is a world-renown aeronautical engineer, aviation pioneer and in my opinion, a business genius: he's designed, built and flown some of the world's most cutting edge civilian & military aircraft as well as spacecraft. And, he's not only one of two people who have successfully flown around the world non-stop, but did it in a plane that he designed and built just for that purpose.

Now, I don't know Mr. Rutan personally, and I have never met him; however, I do know what his 10 tips for success in aviation design and life are, and number seven on his list is:

Keep it simple.

And in my professional opinion, this success tip was always meant to be and should always be the number one tip for making great financial investment choices:

Keep it simple.

Why? Simplicity is the hallmark of genius when it comes to consumer buying decisions as well as financial investment choices.

Yet, and for some bizarre reason, and in particular as it relates to financial investment choices, the Ninety-Nine Percenters are completely obsessed with the complicated: they actually believe and are absolutely convinced that the more complicated and risk laden the financial investment opportunities are, the more profitable the returns will be on that financial investment; and, the cost, much less.

Now, I don't call that genius: I call that absolute stupidity.

And, the One-Percenters would agree with me, because they know that any financial investment choice they engage must conform to Micro Hedge Fund principles: a simplistic and genius way to analyze, evaluate and validate financial investment choice opportunities.

Not surprisingly, the Micro Hedge Fund Matrix enables just that: it enables the Micro Hedge Fund Manager to assess the strength and the suitability of the Object's potential as a financial investment choice. How is this done?

If you recall, at the beginning of this book, I mentioned that we would use the Dress to illustrate the methods, principles, values and virtues that made the Dress an incredible Micro Hedge Fund financial investment choice as well as three other examples to illustrate the power of the Micro Hedge Fund Matrix in action.

That said, the remaining half of this book will be used to achieve this goal. We'll be looking at, and in this order, how the use of the Micro Hedge Matrix model analyzed, evaluated and validated the potential of four financial investment choices:

The Dress;
The Car;
The Home; and,
The Boat

And, after we complete this exercise together, we'll check your pulse and see just how fast it's beating, because at the end of this exercise, if your heart isn't racing with excitement, I'm not sure you can be saved.

The Dress

I am a subscriber to Julien's Auctions, and was notified in advance of their open-to-the-public Auction Event, whereby the Dress, would be auctioned off.

As a professional Micro Hedge Fund Manager I always look for Object opportunities such as these: It is part of my role as a professional to be an expert when it comes to the assets of famous celebrities such as Marilyn Monroe but also other celebrities, whose accomplishments while they lived and whose reputations after they died continue to amaze and captivate audiences, both young and old, throughout the world; and, most likely, will continue to do so until the end of time.

But I digress: let me get back on track.

I was provided with a catalog of all of the items that were to be auctioned off, and lo and behold, there it was: the Dress, which hadn't seen the light of day since it was previously auctioned off in 1999 for 1.26 Million USD. Today, that same 1.26 Million USD would equal $1,818,313.00. For our purposes, we'll round this number down to 1.8 Million USD.

Now let's quickly put you in the shoes of that owner from 1999: you spent 1.26 Million USD to purchase in 1999, which in 2016 dollars equals 1.8 Million USD; and, your fees associated with purchasing the Dress in 1999 was zero dollars.

Now, the auction has come and gone: You've just sold the Dress to an anonymous buyer for 4.8 Million USD. What was your Return on Investment (ROI)?

To calculate it, you simply take the gain of an investment, subtract the cost of the investment, and divide the total by the cost of the investment and then multiple that number by 100. Or:

ROI = (Gains − Cost)/Cost * 100

(4.8 M USD − 1.8 M USD) / 1.8 M USD * 100

ROI = 166%

Congratulations: your investment has paid off handsomely, and in more ways than one.

But we still haven't answered the question, "What made the Dress such an incredible Micro Hedge Fund financial investment choice?

First, the Dress is an Object: remember that all Micro Hedge Fund financial investment choices focus on Objects, not business entities.

Second, the Dress is Valuable, Unique, Powerful and Nostalgic: remember, the financial investment choices of the wealthy and the rich have and will always be driven by their intuitive, instinctive and intrinsic desire to acquire Objects that are Valuable, Unique, Powerful and Nostalgic. But it goes much deeper than that, and this is where a closer examination of the phenomenon is required.

One Percenters know that financial investment choices must only be made in tangible Objects, like the Dress, which represent the lives of significant persons whose own Power, Prestige and Social Standing molded and shaped events, things and places in human history, and that leave us amazed, captivated and spell bound even to this day.

Think about it: what if you could enter the house where Marilyn lived and died? What if you could walk the hallways of that house, or enter into the bedroom where Marilyn spent her last night alive? Wouldn't you feel excited? Wouldn't you feel amazed, captivated or even spell bound?

Think about it: what if you could not only own, but touch the Dress? Wouldn't you feel as if you were connected somehow to the very person who wore the Dress or the very President who made love to that actress? Wouldn't you think that somehow, someway, you were able to go back in time and experience the excitement of what it must have been like to not only have worn the Dress, but actually been "there?"

An Object, any Object that elicits such emotions and enables the owner of that Object to transcend the past, the present and the future is Nostalgic, Powerful, Unique and Valuable. Nostalgic, because the Object empowers the owner with all of the qualities people admire, cherish and adore the most (from the past). Powerful, because the owner experiences a connection and a transformation, because of the life force the Object possesses from the original owner (that person being Powerful, Prestigious and having a high Social Standing, such as Marilyn).

49

Unique, because like Marilyn, it is one of kind: there hasn't been and won't be another Object quite like it, because of the original, "one of a kind" owner who once possessed it. And, Valuable, because in the hands of an owner who has the mindset of the One Percent, that Object will in the mind of the owner as well as in the minds of world, will increase, enhance and redefine the new owners Power, Prestige and Social Standing.

And, if you wanted to become that new owner, what price would you pay for such a Valuable, Unique, Powerful and Nostalgic Object, that is guaranteed to increase your Power, your Prestige and your Social Standing, even if you are "anonymous?"

The answer is 4.8 Million USD.

My highest bid: 3.9 Million USD.

When I received the notification from Julien's, I updated my research and contacted our cooperative's subscribers: I let them know of this incredible opportunity, and outlined the strategy and the tactics that would enable our Micro Hedge Fund to profit handsomely from acquiring the Dress.

I knew beyond a shadow of a doubt that my ROI would be just under 300% if I would have been able to purchase the Dress for 3.9 Million USD. I also knew that a bid over 3.9 Million USD was a losing proposition, short or long term.

How did I know? the Micro Hedge Fund Matrix.

The Car

I purchased my first luxury auto import in 1991: it was a brand new BMW 318is, and it was a phenomenal car! Prior to owning my 318is, I was had been driving a Pontiac Firebird (base model), which I had purchased from a doctor in residency the year before.

But my boss at the time was an admirer of German engineering, and throughout his entire life the only cars that ever gave him any driving pleasure were BMWs. They are well designed, well built, safe and very fast!

And one sunny spring morning, instead of seeing him park into his reserved space in his four-door BMW 745i luxury sedan, this 58 year old executive shows up in his brand new BMW 840ci; and, if you've never seen or driven an 840ci, you don't know what you're missing!!!

But again, I digress.

I couldn't afford a BMW 840ci: when they came out, only celebrities, CEOs and gurus like Tony Robbins purchased them: they were that expensive. But what I could afford was a brand new BMW 318is with a sports package for just under $25,000 dollars; and having test driven one the day after my boss showed up in his 840ci, I was hooked on BMWs. And, after I got my car, I really put that "Ultimate Driving Machine" through its paces.

Immediately thereafter, my Power, my Prestige and my Social standing skyrocketed!!!

My personal life soared...overnight!!! However, it wasn't the car that really made the difference, but rather how I lived and expressed myself as a result of making a very wise consumer buying decision. That decision opened up a whole new level of self-awareness, and elevated my Power, Prestige and Social Standing to a new level that others envied, recognized and respected.

Yes, I had that car for five years; and, would you believe it: in a momentary lapse of reason, I traded it in on a Chevrolet sport utility vehicle. I'm actually embarrassed to admit it, because, if that doesn't show you how completely ass backwards I had become, you need to get your brain checked. God, knows, I sure did!!!

But bad consumer buying decisions and bad financial investment choices lead to significant breakthroughs; and, I got my head screwed on right and rediscovered my true self and put my life back in order after that mistake.

Over time, I forgave myself for letting my BMW 318is go. Years later, I'd search the internet in the hope of finding and purchasing another 1991 BMW 318is just like it, because I did miss the pleasure of driving that make and model; and yes, I was trying to relive the past! What's wrong with that, especially when the past was so pleasurable and rewarding?

And, in 2001, I found one: a 1991 318is for $58,000 dollars. $58,000 dollars!!! It was virtually identical to my original car, except that the seller had upgraded the wheels and tires, added euro-styled body fairings and installed an after-market turbo system.

It looked fast, and I am sure it was fast, but I wasn't fast enough, because when I called the seller that same day to make an offer, the car had already sold the day before. I was floored: the car had only been on the market three days, and already it was gone.

Think about it: without the modifications, a comparable, new model in 2001 dollars was worth only $32,500. And, with the additional $6,500 dollars in upgrades and associated labor costs, that car should have only priced at out $39,000 dollars.

And then, I had an epiphany: I was on to something, and that something would lead me to the creation the Micro Hedge Fund Matrix.

Yes, the 1991 BMW 318is was a fantastic car for a lot of great reasons, and apparently I wasn't the only person who thought so: obviously, I wasn't the only owner of that make and model who had at one time, experienced how Valuable, Unique, Powerful and Nostalgic that make and model would become.

An experiment was now order.

First, locate a 1991 BMW 318is for sale, preferably one in good condition and having none of the upgrades mentioned previously. And, I did: it was, ironically, identical to my 318is, and in fairly good condition. It also had about the same mileage as the 318is that had been sold for $58,000. I purchased this one for $5,100 dollars.

Second, restore the purchased 318is and install the exact upgrades. And, I did: I hired a BMW trained mechanic and body repair specialist, and had them transform this vehicle. By the way, the cost to do this was $12,000 dollars.

Third, advertise the car for sale. I really didn't want to do this, but I had to. And, I listed the car for sale with an asking price of $48,000 dollars.

Now to recap, I had purchased the car for $5,100 dollars, and had it completely restored and updated for $12,000 dollars. I had, in the course of two months spent $17,100 dollars, and was now prepared to sell the car outright for $48,000 dollars.

Three weeks later, the car sold for $46,500 dollars.

What was my ROI?

ROI = (Gains – Cost)/Cost * 100

($46,500 – $17,100) / $17,100 * 100

ROI = 172%

Now, I know what you are thinking...

...*"Who in their right mind would need to purchase a 1991 BMW 318is, that had 6 owners from multiple states and had more than its fair share of accidents, scratches and dents...for $46,500 even after being completely restored and upgraded?"*...

The answer: BMW enthusiasts who race in amateur or Pro-am racing events.

I'm a BMW enthusiast, but I never knew until 2001 how many other BMW enthusiasts raced as amateurs in Pro-am events sponsored by various car clubs in the USA and also overseas. And, I didn't know how many of them used modified 1990 – 1991 BMW 3 Series (318is or 325i) models to compete in these racing events.

But what I also didn't know was how popular these cars were with the "Fast & Furious" crowd on the main streets, because of their ease of modification as well as their ability to maneuver at high speeds. These people don't need to "Tokyo Drift" away their weekends: they WANT to!!! And, they want to, because for these wealthy and rich individuals, the Nostalgia, the Power, the Uniqueness and the Value that this and other vehicles provides them builds their Power, their Prestige and their Social Standing. For them, this consumer buying decision is a fantastic financial investment choice that pays them dividends far beyond money!!!

So, having said that, have you made the Paradigm Shift yet?

The Home

Southern California is the place a lot of people want to be, but for most, they simply can't afford it. Do you know how much homes cost in Southern California (or in Northern California for that matter)? A lot!!! And, the reasons why should be obvious.

In 2006 I was living in Beverly Hills; and, I was living in a very nice condominium, next door to a friend of a friend. That same year, that friend of friend inherited her father's home after he died: it had been built in the early 1960's, and had an unusual reputation, which was known to the locals as well as a lot of wealthy and rich people living in Beverly Hills, Brentwood and Santa Monica. What was this reputation?

Her father had been friends with many famous people, and many of these celebrities and stars during the 60's, 70's and 80's would visit him at his home in Costa Mesa. Some of his friends were more famous than others, but one of his guests was a world renowned singer, swinger, record producer and business tycoon: the legendary Frank Sinatra.

My friend, a television actress, didn't like the house. It was old: it needed major repairs; and, even though it was considered prime real estate (because it commanded an awesome view of the Pacific Ocean), she just didn't want to bother with it or with real estate agents. And, that's when the deluge of calls started coming in: when real estate agents from across the state learned through grape vine that this house might be up for sale, they came running like foxes to the hen house.

She didn't trust many people, but she trusted me, and because she trusted me, she asked me, "What do I do?"

Being the consummate professional, I spent that entire weekend educating her about Micro Hedge Funds and the mindset of the One Percenters. By the end of the weekend, she was transformed! This is what happened next.

First, the property had a first and only mortgage on it for $450,000 dollars. Title was checked, and my friend inherited a home that was free and clear of any leans, etc.

Second, I notified our cooperative's subscribers of this new opportunity and spelled out for them the strategy, tactics and potential, which included set up a new Object Portfolio to create a second mortgage of $350,000 to cover renovations and updates to the property.

Third, with the Portfolio established, and during the course of the next six months, the home was completely renovated and updated (and I might add with some gadgets that would make James Bond drool). The cost of the renovations equaled $350,000 dollars.

Forth, once the renovations were completed, I borrowed two, 2-year old Bentleys, and put them in the garage. The cost of-this was zero, because my friend who sells them didn't have any space on his lot at the time for them, and he needed a safe place to keep them until some space on his lot opened up.

Fifth, I snapped some very cool pictures of the entire home, and placed those pictures on the internet (where, exactly, I won't say: that's privileged information).

Two months and three weeks after the renovations were completed the home sold for 1.7 Million USD.

At closing, proceeds were split fifty – fifty: approximately $450,000 dollars each.

ROI: 112.5%

Are you beginning to see how Objects turn out to be incredible Micro Hedge Fund financial investment choice opportunities?

The Boat

The wealthy and the rich love the water; and, if you don't believe me, all you have to do is look at the sailboats and yachts in their possession today. These gigantic, trans-oceanic vessels are becoming the primary homes of the One Percent, because when it comes to Dignity Building, there are fewer consumer buying decisions that achieve this so elegantly and so well.

Yes, it is a small world, and, because I'm a proven quantity when it comes to Dignity Building, I always have yacht brokers trying to help me accelerate my growth process. Like most people I don't like to be pushed or hounded: when I'm ready for the next level, the transition will be as natural as taking my next breath.

But I have an acquaintance who is a go-getter: he's a yacht broker, who through our many conversations together has become familiar with my preferences. And, when it comes to sail boats, my number one preference is Beneteau.

One day, he emails me: "You have got to look at this boat! It's a dealer leftover from the previous model year, and its listed $100,000 dollars below retail."

That caught my eye. And, after I read the attached brochure, and found out that all of the factory warranties would be honored just as if the boat had sold new at the retail price, I knew exactly what I had to do.

First, I did my research on the make and model, because it was a first generation sailboat design. And, I did that: I got all of my facts and figures. Everything, from forecasted maintenance costs to annual insurance requirements to where I could park the beast and how much slip fees would cost me.

Second, I checked resale values: this make and model was new to the sailing world, and many simply had not changed hands. But when I learned that the depreciation statistics were excellent and that the model was one of only a handful that had appreciated in value, I was satisfied.

Third, I sent a FLASH email to our cooperative's subscribers who are the most active when it comes to financial investment choices, and provided exact details about the deal: our entrance strategy, our exit strategy and the potential ROI when the deal was closed.

Fourth, with the Portfolio created, we took a 60-day option on contract to purchase the boat for its retail price of $765,000 and added the $100,000 discount to the option. This brought the price of the boat to $665,000 dollars. A non-refundable deposit of 15% of the sales price was required (we negotiated that down to 5%, which was returned when the deal closed).

Fifth, we remarketed the boat at a sales price of $795,000.

Three weeks after the remarking effort, we received an overseas offer for the boat of $725,000 dollars. We countered with an offer to sell for $765,000.

They countered with a final offer to purchase for $745,000. And, we accepted their offer subject to appraisal and inspection.

A contract was signed, and three weeks after the appraisal and inspection were complete the boat was sold, as is, for $745,000 dollars.

ROI = 12%

Now, you may be thinking that 12% isn't much, but when was the last time one of your investments made an ROI of 12% and so quickly?

THE MATRIX RELOADED

Even though the Car financial investment choice was made prior to the establishment of the Micro Hedge Fund concept and model, it was the experiment required to prove that the concept is real and works. And, like all of the experiments that followed after the Car (although the Objects were not all automobiles), each and every experiment performed as expected: flawlessly.

And, even though the Dress, as an Object, wasn't acquired, the use of the Micro Hedge Fund Matrix provided the knowledge and wisdom to know "when to start bidding", "how much to bid" and "when not to bid."

Whereas, the Boat (in its Portfolio) and the Home (in its separate Portfolio) were shining examples of how the Micro Hedge Fund Matrix could validate potential and did earn a combined return on investment of 124.5% the same year.

ROI = 124.5%

Now, if you would have been a cooperative share member of the Micro Hedge Fund at that time, and having opted to participate in the Portfolios established for the Boat and the Home, for every dollar deposited, you would have realized a $2.45 return on investment.

Ask yourself: when was the last time you made a consumer buying decision and a financial investment choice that provided a return on investment of 124.5%?

It is true: there are few, very few, consumer buying decisions and financial investment choices that yield that type of return of investment in one year, or two years, or three years or four; however, when Objects which are identified, analyzed, evaluated and validated using the Micro Hedge Fund Matrix, the potential to achieve significant returns on investment far exceed any other investment strategy, bar none.

And, I like to call this the "Financial certainty of success", which by the way is our firms copyrighted and trademarked logo, slogan and motto, so please don't try and use it.

So it begs to question, how does the Micro Hedge Fund Matrix actually work?

How it works is a proprietary and trade secret: I cannot and will not provide specific details regarding the mathematics, equations and formulas that have been developed in order to use the Matrix to create the "Financial certainty of success." However, what I have and already done in this book is provided you with the method behind the genius.

"How so", you ask?

Let's reload the Matrix with binary numbers, and afterwards, I'll explain.

THE MATRIX			
Emotion / Object	Power	Prestige	Social Standing
Valuable	1011101	0000110	1100111
Unique	0101011	0101000	1100001
Powerful	0100001	0100100	0000010
Nostalgic	0010101	0000000	1011011

There are nine fields within the Matrix, and I want you to think of each field as representing what I call a "Pyramid of Profitability." Nine fields: nine Pyramids of Profitability.

I've loaded each field with binary numbers: these numbers represent a powerful, weighted value based upon simplistic but proprietary mathematical calculations and sub-calculations, that when aggregated, enables our firm to evaluate not only an Objects performance potential, but also the short and long term implications of that Objects performance in relation to other Objects / Portfolios within the Micro Hedge Fund.

Not only does the Matrix provide a verifiable Go / No Go consumer buying decision but also provides a verifiable Go / No Go financial investment choice based upon Emotion and Object factors (which we have defined previously, and are listed in the Matrix).

Consequently, and for our firm, our "method to the genius" is like the original formula for Coca Cola: highly guarded and secret. Yes, some people have tried to reverse engineer our "formula", but they simply can't create an equal or superior result: in fact, they fall terribly short each and every time.

So, where does this leave us?

The One Percenters Pill of Choice

I'm not a fan of the movie, "The Matrix" or any of its sequels, but I chose to borrow from the film its "Red Pill" versus the "Blue Pill" metaphor, because, in my opinion, it illustrates very well how and what I want to communicate to you as we approach the end of this literary experience together.

Briefly, and to explain to the reader who may be unfamiliar with the movie or its metaphors, in the film, the main character ("Neo") is visited by a mysterious man named Morpheus, who recognizes that Neo's consciousness is beginning to awaken and question all that he is and all that he does as well as the life he is leading.

During the meeting, Morpheus explains to Neo that the world he is living in may appear real, but it is actually a by-product of something called the Matrix. And, he offers Neo an incredible opportunity during this meeting: a choice between taking a red pill and a blue pill.

The red pill would allow Neo to escape from the Matrix and into the real world, therefore living the "truth of reality" even though it is a harsher, more difficult life.

Or, the blue pill, which would leave Neo stuck in the pretend world, where the mundane and the mediocre live.

To paraphrase Morpheus: "You take the blue pill and you remain a member of the Ninety-Nine Percenters. You take the red pill, and you become a One Percenter, and I show you just how deep the Rabbit Hole goes."

Can you guess the pill of choice for the One-Percenters, who own ninety-nine percent of the world's wealth and riches?

Most of you who are reading this book now have been living in a world of make believe: you've been born into a world that seems normal, but deep down within your spirit and your soul, you have this uneasy feeling: this pang in your gut that questions how you are living, or in other words, why you are only existing. You don't feel like you're alive: truly alive. And, you don't feel like you're truly aware of your God-given abilities, gifts, skills and talents or how to utilize them to fulfill your potential and grow as a human being.

Many of you continue to be bombarded daily with disinformation, misinformation and useless information, which keeps you dumb and numb: it is information overload ad infinitum, and it is preventing you from learning, understanding, believing, embracing and applying the truth about how to properly gain Power, Prestige and Social Standing through appropriate consumer buying decisions as well as building wealth and riches through creative financial investment choices, which are characterized as being Valuable, Unique, Powerful and Nostalgic.

Do you want to know how far the Rabbit Hole goes? If your answer is "Yes", then I'm your guide and our Micro Hedge Fund is the vessel that will take you on this eyes-wide open journey into the real world of Dignity Building.

Now, it is time to check out your bonus.

GET YOUR $700.00 MICRO HEDGE FUND BONUS!

Carefully remove this page from your book, and clearly print your contact information in the box below. Then, mail this page via U.S. Postal Service First Class Mail (or the equivalent if you are mailing it from outside the USA) to the address underneath:

Name:

Address:

City, State, Zip Code:

Contact Phone Number:

Email Address:

Aufidena Financial
1205 Johnson Ferry Road
Suite 136-212
Marietta, Georgia 30068

You'll receive via email a voucher with a code number and instructions to register for one of our Micro Hedge Fund Seminars: a $1,495 USD value, discounted to $795 for owners of this book only. At the seminar, you'll discover how you can invest in secured, insured and collateralized Micro Hedge Fund Object Portfolios, and learn about the unlimited potential of Micro Hedge Fund initiatives.

And for those of you who want to go deeper into the Rabbit Hole, you'll be introduced to a very unique offer to become a Micro Hedge Fund Manager.

www.ingramcontent.com/pod-product-compliance
Lightning Source LLC
Chambersburg PA
CBHW061207180526
45170CB00002B/997